To: Vayl

I am dedicating this book to my two granddaughters: Jordan and Abi.

Ken Ralls
8.3 - 2013

Ken Ralls, 2011

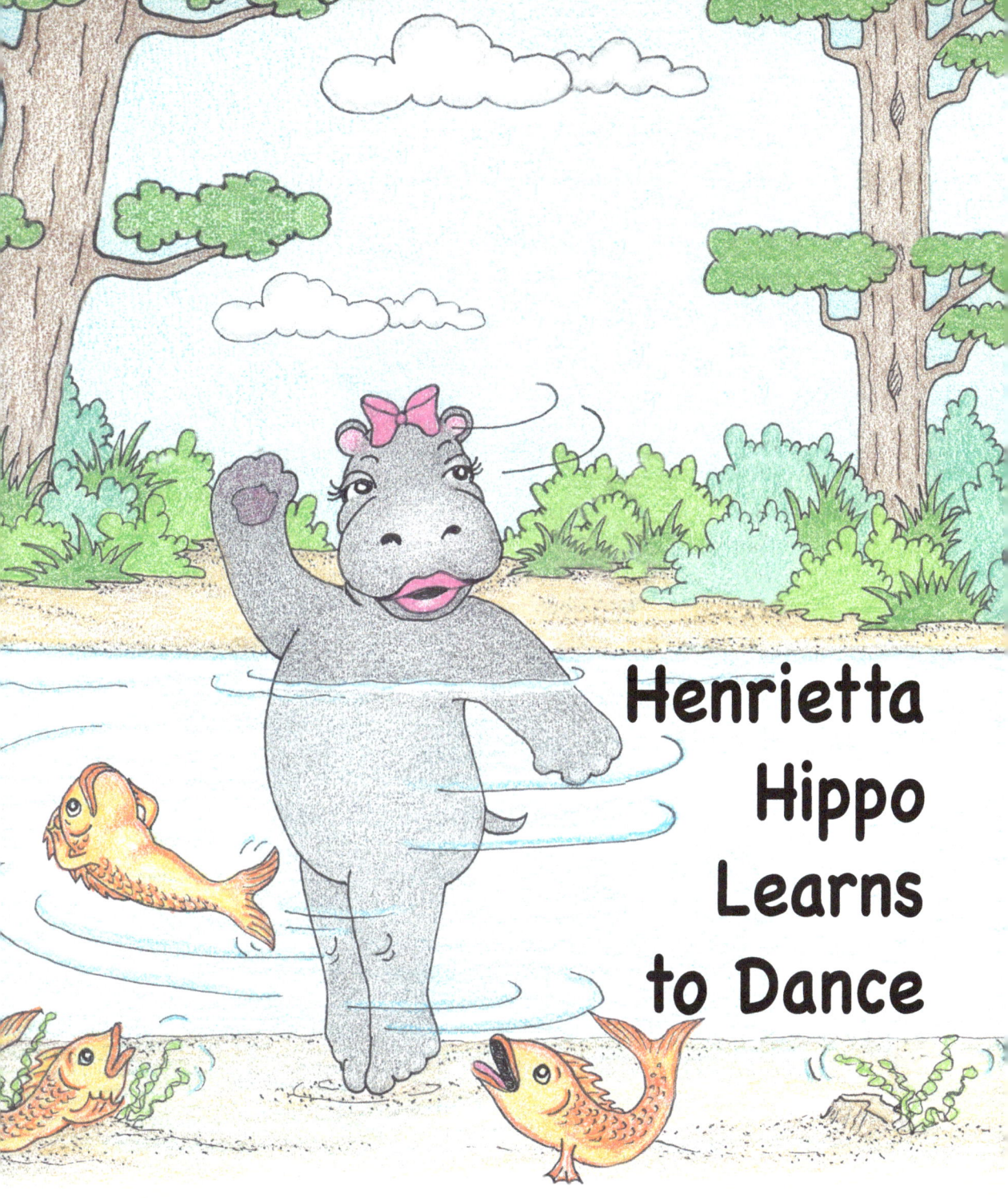

Henrietta Hippo Learns to Dance

Written by Ken Ralls

Illustrated by LaVonia Corbin McQuitty

Henrietta Hippo Learns to Dance

Copyright © 2011
Ken Ralls

The Scribe's Closet Publications
702 South Missouri
Macon, MO 63552
www.thescribesclosetpublications.com

All rights reserved.
This book may not be reproduced in whole or in part
or transmitted in any form without written permission
from the publisher, except by a reviewer
who may quote a brief passage in a review:
nor may any part of the book be reproduced,
stored in a retrieval system, or transmitted in any form
or by any means, electronic, mechanical, photocopied,
recorded, or other without written permission
from the publisher.

First Edition, 2011
ISBN 978-0-9832570-4-2

Second Edition, 2013
ISBN 978-0-9884125-3-8

Printed in The United States of America

Henrietta had dreamed of being a ballerina since she was five years old.

"Today I am going to start dancing!"
Henrietta decided.

She walked into the river,
where the water was really deep.

Standing on one toe,
her head barely escaped the water.

Henrietta began to twirl around and around on one toe.

Oh, this was fun!

"La, la-la-la-la, la!" she sang as she spun round and round.

Zelda Zebra came down to the river for a drink.

"La, la-la-la-la, la!" Henrietta was singing and whirling in the water.

"Why are you singing?" asked Zelda Zebra.

"I am going to be a ballerina!" Henrietta declared.

She kept spinning round and round.

"Ha, ha, ha! Hippos can't dance!" cried Zelda. "You will never be a ballerina!"

"Oh, yes I will! La, la-la-la-la, la." Henrietta kept twirling round and round.

Every day, Henrietta went down to the river.
She practiced standing on her toes
as she rotated in the water.

After many days of practice,
Henrietta was whirling in the river
with her head and shoulders out of the water.

Ella Elephant came to the river to bathe.
She saw Henrietta and said,
"Hippos can't dance!"

"Maybe you can't dance, but I will!"
Henrietta declared. "I'm going to be a ballerina."

Ella went through the jungle, telling all her friends that Henrietta wanted to be a ballerina.

They laughed at her dream.

Henrietta kept going to the river every day.
She stood on her toes and spun in the water.

Every day she practiced,
and every day she got better at dancing.
Henrietta was learning to be a ballerina.

Many days later, Henrietta was twirling around in the river. The water was just up to her tummy.

Lena Hyena had heard about the dancing hippo, so she came to the river to watch. Lena laughed so much that she fell in the sand by the river.

She ran through the jungle,
stopping everyone she met.

"Henrietta Hippo thinks she can be a ballerina!"

They laughed and laughed.
But Henrietta kept practicing.

"La, la-la-la-la, la." Henrietta was spinning in the river where the water was just to her knees.

Gloria Gorilla came to pick leaves for her dinner. "Hippos don't dance," she said, watching Henrietta.

"Oh, but I will!" Henrietta kept twirling. "La, la-la-la-la, la."

One day Henrietta went to the river,
but she did not go into the water.

She rose up on one toe and began dancing.

"La, la-la-la-la, la," she danced
up and down the river bank on her toes.

All the animals came to watch. They were amazed as Henrietta danced round and round on her toes in the sand.

"Henrietta can dance!" they cheered.

"Yes, I can! La, la-la-la-la, la," Henrietta twirled on her toes.

**The next morning,
little Ruthie Rhino walked into the river
and stood on one toe...**

Author Ken Ralls

Ken is a retired teacher, active author, and paper mache artist. His creation of a dancing hippo led to Henrietta's story. He can't believe his good fortune at finding such a talented illustrator and expert editor for this project.

The five novels in Ken's **McKay's Island** series deal with the adventures of a military family that homesteads an island in the Pacific.

His **Dandelion Acres** series of novels center around a writer's retreat center in Clarence, Missouri.

Ken's books are available online from his website, **www.freewebs.com/rallsworks** or from Susan White of The Scribe's Closet Publications at **www.thescribesclosetpublications.com.**

Illustrator LaVonia Corbin McQuitty

Lavonia (Sammy) is an artist, a poet, and children's book author and illustrator, who began drawing when she was three years old. Sammy has been practicing now for 63 years.

Sammy's portraits of famous people have been featured in **Country Weekly Magazine.**

Besides her own books, (**A Little Dog's Tale; A Trip to Pucky Huddle; Patches, A Doll's Story**), LaVonia has illustrated books for Nashville singer-songwriter Terry Smith (**The Little Brown Dog and The Little Green Frog; A Christmas Stocking's Story**), Linda Hoff Clement (**Hit the Road Mister Monster**), and Susan White (**Jesus Does Good Things**).

Sammy's books are available from her publisher, Susan White of The Scribe's Closet Publications at **www.thescribesclosetpublications.com**.

CPSIA information can be obtained at www.ICGtesting.com
Printed in the USA
LVOW012311100613

337926LV00001B/1/P